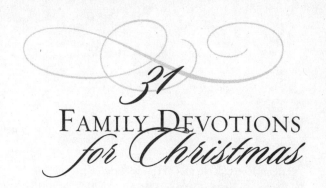

31
FAMILY DEVOTIONS
for Christmas

D1539336

MariLee Parrish

BARBOUR
PUBLISHING

ISBN 978-1-60260-024-9

Published by Barbour Publishing, Inc., P.O. Box 719,
Uhrichsville, Ohio 44683, www.barbourbooks.com

*Our mission is to publish and distribute inspirational products
offering exceptional value and biblical encouragement to the
masses.*

Member of the
Evangelical Christian
Publishers Association

Printed in the United States of America.

Dear Friends,

As many of you do, I *love* Christmas! From the Thanksgiving Day Parade all the way to New Year's Day, I love everything about the Christmas season! To me, Christmas isn't just one day to prepare for, and it certainly isn't just for children, as we so often hear. Christmas is an entire season of hope and love and joy! As Christians, we should be living out the spirit of Christmas every day of the year. However, we often get caught up in the hustle and bustle, and before you know it, Christmas is over and we end up stressed and tired with a pile of bills hanging over our heads.

Many of us are guilty of trying too hard to plan the perfect Christmas. This year, why not strive to spend more time together as a family, reflecting on the true meaning of Christmas rather than worrying over organizing a flawless holiday? This daily devotional contains family devotions, stress-free tips, family activities, recipes, and more to help you do just that. Have fun, and merry Christmas!

With love and many Christmas blessings,
MariLee Parrish

24 Days until Christmas

Let the peace of Christ rule in your hearts,
since as members of one body you were
called to peace. And be thankful.
COLOSSIANS 3:15

Thanksgiving is over, but let's not forget to carry the mind-set of thankfulness into the Christmas season. Be grateful and let peace permeate your thoughts and actions this Christmas. Instead of beginning this month worrying about money or gifts or filling your schedule to the brim with every imaginable holiday activity, ask the Lord to rule in your heart this holiday season.

Father, Thank You for the upcoming holiday season.
Thank You for sending Your Son for us. Help me
to keep my focus on You this Christmas and to make
this a time of love, hope, and joy for my family and
friends. Allow us to bless someone in need this year.
As I begin planning for Christmas, let my heart
be set on worshipping You this season and not
expecting the "perfect" Christmas. Amen.

Family Activity

It is a tradition in many homes to find the annual Christmas tree the day after Thanksgiving. Putting up the tree can top the list as one of the greatest family activities of all time no matter when you choose to accomplish the wonderful task. Find a tree farm that will let you cut down your own. Many places will take you into the woods on a wagon or in a sleigh and serve hot chocolate or other special treats.

Stress-free Tip

To avoid a major hassle removing your lights after Christmas, start at the base of your tree and work up. Wear heavy gardening gloves and long sleeves when putting lights up and taking them down so that you don't get pricked by the tree or get a rash. When you remove the lights after Christmas, remember to start at the top and work down.

Banana Chocolate Chip Coffee Cake

1⅓ cups sugar
1 cup sour cream
¼ cup butter or
    margarine, softened
4 eggs
2 cups flour
½ teaspoon salt

1 teaspoon baking
    soda
3 to 4 medium
    bananas, very ripe,
    mashed
2 teaspoons vanilla
2 cups milk chocolate
    chips

Heat oven to 375 degrees. Cream sugar, sour cream, butter, and eggs. Stir in flour, salt, and baking soda. Add bananas and vanilla; mix well. Stir in chocolate chips. Spread in greased 9x11-inch pan. Bake 35 minutes. Cool in pan.

Since, then, you have been raised with Christ,
set your hearts on things above, where Christ is
seated at the right hand of God. Set your minds
on things above, not on earthly things.
COLOSSIANS 3:1–2

A Christ-centered holiday begins when we set our
hearts on things above. Decide today that you will
not let the commercialism of the holiday spoil the
simple message of God's love for us. Fix your heart
on the true meaning of Christmas: God sent His
only Son to earth so that we could be with Him for
eternity! If you do not know Jesus Christ as your
personal Savior, take time right now to ask Him to
come into your life and forgive your sins. You will
never experience more joy in this world than when
you allow the love of God to inhabit your soul.

Father, thank You for loving us and sending
Your Son into the world to save us from our sins so
that we can be with You forever. Help us to set
our hearts and minds on You today and
always. In Jesus' name, amen.

Family Activity

Make your own Advent calendar. Spend time as a family each day counting down the days until Christmas. One way to do this is to make a paper chain, adding one link every morning and using it to decorate your tree on Christmas Eve.

Stress-free Tip

Start making lists of everything you will need for the holidays. These may include a baking list, a craft list, and a gift-giving list. Keep a special notebook with you at all times so that when you remember something you need to do, you can write it down right away. It's also a good idea to mark your calendar with each event to which you will need to bring a dish or dessert. That way you won't forget and have to scramble for a store-bought item at the last minute.

OATMEAL SCOTCHIES

¾ cup butter, softened
¾ cup sugar
¾ cup brown sugar
2 eggs
1 teaspoon vanilla
1½ cups flour

1 teaspoon baking soda
1 teaspoon cinnamon
½ teaspoon salt
3 cups rolled oats
2 cups butterscotch
   chips

Preheat oven to 375 degrees. Beat butter and sugars together. Add eggs and vanilla, beating well. Stir together dry ingredients with a wire whisk until well blended. Gradually add to creamy mixture and stir until blended. Stir in the oats and the butterscotch chips. Drop by spoonfuls onto an ungreased cookie sheet. Bake 7 to 9 minutes until edges begin to brown. Store in sealed container. Makes about 4 dozen.

> "Be careful not to do your 'acts of righteousness' before men, to be seen by them. If you do, you will have no reward from your Father in heaven. So when you give to the needy, do not announce it with trumpets, as the hypocrites do in the synagogues and on the streets, to be honored by men. I tell you the truth, they have received their reward in full. But when you give to the needy, do not let your left hand know what your right hand is doing, so that your giving may be in secret. Then your Father, who sees what is done in secret, will reward you."
>
> MATTHEW 6:1–4

Christmas is all about giving from the heart. God gave us His Son! Let's give of ourselves to one another as an act of worship to our heavenly Father. Take some time with your family to think about what you can do for someone else this holiday season. Begin your December with the spirit of giving, and cultivate it as much as possible throughout the month. Presents and parties are fun for a while, but the true spirit of giving lasts for eternity.

Father, allow us to honor You in all that we do this season. Let us bless someone else in need this Christmas for the purpose of glorifying Your name alone. Amen.

Family Activity

Contact your church and find out what ministries or charities your church is supporting this year. Then get involved! Many churches participate in Operation Christmas Child, an outreach project that involves filling shoe boxes with toys and school supplies for children in need all over the world. Have each child in your family fill a shoe box for a needy child. They will have fun picking out gifts for someone else, and the project helps to keep the focus on others. To find out more about Operation Christmas Child, go to www. samaritanspurse.org.

Stress-free Tip

Find a large jar and start saving all of your family's loose change. Everyone can contribute. Next December you will have plenty of money saved to help someone in need.

Extraordinary
Ohio Buckeyes

1 cup creamy peanut
  butter
½ cup (1 stick) butter
  or margarine
1¾ cups powdered sugar

2 cups semisweet, milk,
  or white chocolate
  chips
Toothpicks for dipping

Line cookie sheets with wax paper and set aside. Mix peanut butter and butter until creamy. Add sugar a little at a time. Refrigerate for 30 minutes. Roll peanut butter mixture into 1-inch balls. Place on wax paper and freeze for 30 minutes or until firm. In microwave-safe dish, melt chocolate chips in microwave on high for 30 seconds. Stir. Repeat until chips are melted. Do not scorch. Insert toothpicks into frozen peanut butter balls and dip balls in chocolate. Let cool on wax paper. Store in cool place. Makes about 100 buckeyes.

"In the same way, let your light shine before men,
that they may see your good deeds and
praise your Father in heaven."
MATTHEW 5:16

Jesus tells us that everything we do for others pleases
God. Let others see Christ shining through you!
Sometimes our good deeds go unnoticed by people,
but don't let this stop you. Ask God to show you how
you can bless another person without getting noticed
today. Maybe you could secretly shovel the driveway
of an elderly neighbor or help with household chores
without anyone knowing. If we're doing everything
for the glory of God, it won't matter if others notice
or not.

Father, let all that I do please You today. Let Your
light shine through me so that others can see that
You are real and that You are working in my
heart. In Jesus' name, amen.

Family Activity

Purchase mini Christmas trees and let each child decorate his or her own. Put the trees in bedrooms, bathrooms, or anywhere that could use an extra touch of Christmas. Maybe even put one in the garage or barn to brighten the day of someone working hard. Younger children can make their own garlands from construction paper or string popcorn or cranberries. Have some hot chocolate and cookies on hand, and everyone will want to join in the fun!

Stress-free Tip

Make sure to have plenty of extension cords when you decorate with lights. Purchase any additional lights or decorations you might need this year. Don't worry if your home doesn't look picture perfect. Your children will have fun decorating in their own way.

Chocolate Drop Cookies

½ cup shortening
2 squares unsweetened
    baking chocolate
2 eggs
1 cup sugar
½ teaspoon vanilla
1⅓ cups flour

Preheat oven to 400 degrees. Melt shortening and chocolate together in medium saucepan. Remove from heat. Beat eggs; add sugar and whisk together well. Add melted chocolate mixture, vanilla, and flour. Mix well. Drop by heaping tablespoons on cookie sheet. Bake for 6 minutes.

20 DAYS UNTIL *Christmas*

*Love the LORD your God with all your heart and
with all your soul and with all your strength. These
commandments that I give you today are to be upon
your hearts. Impress them on your children. Talk about
them when you sit at home and when you walk along
the road, when you lie down and when you get up. Tie
them as symbols on your hands and bind them on
your foreheads. Write them on the doorframes
of your houses and on your gates.*
DEUTERONOMY 6:5–9

The holidays are a wonderful time to remember and
talk about our journey to faith. It is very important
for our children and our families to hear how we
came to know Christ and what the gift of God's Son
means to us. Take a moment to have all family members
share what God is doing in their lives.

*Dear Father, thank You for calling each of us to be
Your child. We are so thankful that You love us and
take care of us. Help us not only to share our faith
with all of those around us, but to live out
our faith each day. Amen.*

Family Activity

After dinner one evening, share memories of Christmases past. Talk about favorite ornaments on the tree and where they came from. Tell about your favorite Christmas as a child or special traditions you remember. You and your children will enjoy hearing what each family member has considered special or memorable in the past.

Stress-free Tip

As you talk about your favorite family traditions, make a list of what each family member considers most important or fun. Have your local newspaper handy and look for any special events coming up. Decide as a family what you would like to do this month and put it on the calendar.

Chocolate-Drizzled Kettle Corn

2–3 bags of microwave
   kettle corn
½ cup chocolate chips
   (milk chocolate or semisweet)
Red and green sugars (optional)

Pop bags of microwave kettle corn and place popped popcorn in a large baking pan. In microwave-safe dish, melt chocolate chips in microwave on high for 30 seconds. Stir. Repeat until chips are melted. Dip a fork into melted chocolate and drizzle chocolate over kettle corn. If desired, sprinkle with colored sugars for a festive touch. Let cool completely. Break apart and store in decorative bags.

*"Therefore, whoever humbles himself like this
child is the greatest in the kingdom of heaven."*
MATTHEW 18:4

"Christmas is just for children." How many times
have we heard that awful phrase? Don't believe it!
Christmas is for children of any age! Jesus asks us to
come to Him with childlike faith. Do you remember the excitement you had as a child waiting for
Christmas morning? Do you remember your faith
as a child? Do you remember when you believed that
God could do anything if you simply asked Him?
The truth is that God is the same yesterday, today,
and forever. Come to Christ this Christmas with the
faith of a little child.

*Heavenly Father, help us to humble ourselves and
come to You always with faith like a child. Help us to
know and believe that You are the God of miracles—
yesterday, today, and forever. Amen.*

Family Activity

Hold a family card-making party. Compile some pictures from throughout the year with captions. Then make color copies to include in your cards. Little ones can help apply address labels or stuff envelopes. Turn on some Christmas music and make this a fun time.

Stress-free Tip

As Christmas cards come in the mail, hang them on a door frame or string them with ribbon from a banister. Spend time as a family praying for the special people who sent you Christmas greetings.

OLD-FASHIONED WALNUT BALLS

1 cup butter	½ teaspoon salt
⅓ cup brown sugar	1½ cups finely chopped
1 teaspoon vanilla	walnuts
2 cups flour	Powdered sugar

Preheat oven to 375 degrees. Cream butter, sugar, and vanilla until fluffy. Sift flour and salt together; add to creamed mixture. Mix well; stir in walnuts. Shape dough into walnut-sized balls. Bake on ungreased cookie sheet for 12 to 15 minutes. Remove from cookie sheet. When still warm but cool enough to handle, roll in powdered sugar. Makes about 4 dozen.

18 DAYS UNTIL *Christmas*

And Mary said: "My soul glorifies the Lord
and my spirit rejoices in God my Savior."
LUKE 1:46–47

Nobody likes to wait. As Mary waited for the birth of her son, she worshipped God. How many of us worship while we are waiting on the Lord? We'll have a lot of waiting to do this month. When you find yourself stuck in line at the mall or caught in the middle of a traffic jam, don't get upset. Worship. Thank God for all His blessings to you. Pray for your family. Pray for the frustrated cashier at the counter. Psalm 37:7 says, "Be still before the LORD and wait patiently for him." Take some time to get your focus off yourself and your circumstances and just worship the Lord.

Dear Lord, let my spirit rejoice in You today.
Help me to think of You and be joyful when
I have to wait this month. Amen.

Family Activity

Plan a winter picnic. On a snowy day, prepare a lunch and warm drinks, pack everything into the car with some blankets, and set off for the park. Bundle up while you eat and have a blast playing in the snow. If you don't have snow where you live, plan an indoor picnic on the living room floor or in front of the fireplace.

Stress-free Tip

Stash several Christmas CDs in your car to keep you in the Christmas spirit while driving to work or school.

Easy Microwave Fudge

3 cups semisweet chocolate
   chips
1 (14 ounce) can sweetened
   condensed milk
1 teaspoon vanilla

In large microwave-safe bowl, combine chocolate chips and sweetened condensed milk. Microwave on high for 2 minutes. Stir in vanilla. Line 8x8-inch pan with wax paper; pour fudge mixture into pan. Refrigerate until firm.

Variations:

For chocolate walnut fudge, add ½ cup chopped walnuts after vanilla.

For peppermint fudge, add ½ teaspoon peppermint flavoring (not oil). Press 3 crushed candy canes on top of fudge before refrigerating.

17 DAYS UNTIL *Christmas*

*The crucible for silver and the furnace for gold,
but the LORD tests the heart.*
PROVERBS 17:3

Too often Christmas becomes all about the presents. Silver, gold, shiny, and new. The more expensive and beautiful, the better—or so we might think. God's Word tells us that material things are not important. They don't last. God is concerned with the state of our hearts, and that is what we should be concerned about, too. Don't worry if you aren't loaded with extra money to spend on extravagant gifts this year. A homemade gift or heartfelt deed means much more than any store-bought item.

*Dear Father, help me to remember that You are
concerned with the state of my heart and not
the amount of money I spend this year. Amen.*

Family Activity

Visit a nursing home as a family. Call ahead and find out how many residents live there. Take them inexpensive little gifts, homemade items, or fruit. Younger children can color some pictures to give away. Talk with the senior residents, and you just might make a few new friends. Join them in singing holiday carols or playing a game or two.

Stress-free Tip

Help de-stress your church's staff. During Christmas break, call your church's secretary and ask if your family can help around the church. Many churches have little jobs that anyone in the family can do: for example, pencil sharpening, bathroom cleanup, or envelope stuffing and stamping.

Old-Fashioned Preserve Thumbprints

1 (8 ounce) package
  cream cheese, softened
¾ cup softened butter
1 cup powdered sugar
2¼ cups flour
½ teaspoon baking soda
½ cup pecans
½ teaspoon vanilla
Strawberry and peach
  fruit preserves

Beat cream cheese, butter, and sugar until smooth. Add flour and soda; mix well. Add pecans and vanilla. Mix well; chill dough for at least 30 minutes. Preheat oven to 350 degrees. Shape dough into 1-inch balls. Place on ungreased cookie sheet. Press your thumb in the middle of each cookie; fill with about 1 teaspoon preserves. Bake 14 to 16 minutes or until light golden brown. Cool on wire rack. Makes about 3 dozen.

16 DAYS UNTIL *Christmas*

> *Jesus replied, "What is impossible*
> *with men is possible with God."*
> LUKE 18:27

What a wonderful time of the year to be reminded that our God is the God of the impossible! Often family issues arise around the holidays. The stress of the season can cause personalities to clash and bring out the worst in us if we aren't careful. Pray for your family. Pray that God would mend any broken relationships. Listen for God's prompting. If you have family members who are hard to get along with, go to them and talk things through. Our great God can heal even the most difficult and seemingly irreparable relationships!

Dear Jesus, thank You for my family. Thank You that
I have so many relatives who love me. Show me
how to love them the way You want me to.
In Jesus' name, amen.

Family Activity

Organize a baking day. Invite friends or family over and bake all day long. Little ones can measure ingredients or have a table set up specifically for them to decorate cutout cookies. Freeze anything that can't be kept until Christmas. Pick a day to deliver these goodies to your friends and neighbors.

Stress-free Tip

If you don't have time to bake several different kinds of cookies, make five dozen of one kind and have a cookie exchange. Invite five friends to bake five dozen of their choice of cookie and host a get-together. Each friend will take home five dozen assorted cookies. If you invite ten friends and make ten dozen cookies, then you will have ten different kinds of cookies!

Vickie's Creamy Cranberry (or Blueberry) Bread

8 ounces cream cheese, softened
1 cup butter
1½ cups sugar
1½ teaspoons vanilla
4 eggs

2¼ cups flour, divided
1½ teaspoons baking powder
½ teaspoon salt
2 cups fresh cranberries or frozen blueberries

Heat oven to 350 degrees. Mix cream cheese, butter, sugar, and vanilla until smooth. Add eggs one at a time, mixing well after each addition. Combine 2 cups flour, baking powder, and salt. Gradually add to butter mixture. Mix ¼ cup flour with cranberries and fold into batter by hand. Batter will be thick. Spoon into 2 greased loaf pans. Bake for 65 to 70 minutes. Let cool in pan for 5 minutes; then cool on wire rack.

15 DAYS UNTIL *Christmas*

*"If you obey my commands, you will remain in my love,
just as I have obeyed my Father's commands and remain
in his love. I have told you this so that my joy may
be in you and that your joy may be complete."*
JOHN 15:10–11

Christmas is a season of joy—joy to the world! Joy
that comes from knowing the love of Christ and the
hope that brings to each of us. Even in difficult times
we can remain in His love and experience the joy of
knowing Him. Focusing on others is a way that your
family can experience the joy of giving. True joy is
found when we look outside of ourselves and focus
on Christ and those around us.

*Dear God, thank You for bringing us true joy.
Help us to obey all of Your commands. Give us
the desire to know You more. Amen.*

Family Activity

Go caroling! Join a group from your church or a local group, or gather a group of your friends and head out on your own. Sing in your neighborhood or go to some homes of elderly people and take them fruit baskets or handmade Christmas greetings. You don't need to have a voice like an angel to bring a smile to someone's face through song.

Stress-free Tip

Set up a wrapping table with scissors, tape, pens, markers, bows, and gift tags. Let the little ones help with the gifts they can wrap. You could also let the kids make their own wrapping paper. Stop by your local newspaper office and ask for end rolls of blank newsprint, or buy a large roll of plain white paper. Set out red and green crayons, markers, and paint, and let the children get to work.

PETER'S TREATS

1 cup butter, softened (do not substitute)	1 teaspoon vanilla
1 cup powdered sugar	1¼ cups flour
Dash salt	1 cup quick oats
	Chocolate star candies

Cream together butter, sugar, and vanilla. Stir in flour, oats, and salt. Shape dough into 2 rolls. Wrap and seal in waxed paper. Chill at least 2 hours. Preheat oven to 350 degrees. Cut dough into ¼-inch slices and place on ungreased cookie sheets. Top each with a chocolate star. Bake for 10 to 12 minutes.

14 DAYS UNTIL *Christmas*

> *"But when you pray, go into your room, close*
> *the door and pray to your Father, who is unseen.*
> *Then your Father, who sees what*
> *is done in secret, will reward you."*
>
> MATTHEW 6:6

Secrets are so much fun at Christmas! From packages hidden in closets and under beds, to stockings filled with special treats, there's always something unexpected to experience. Jesus' birth was an unexpected gift, too. Sure, the Jews were looking for the Messiah to come, but nobody expected the King of kings to come as a baby—or even more surprising, in a stable! The good news is that Jesus' birth wasn't kept a secret for long. That same night angels shouted the secret from the heavens, and shepherds shared the news with everyone they met. How can you share this surprise with someone who doesn't know the secret yet?

Dear heavenly Father, thank You for making the birth
of Your Son an exciting and unexpected gift. Help
us to share unexpected gifts with others, too. Amen.

Family Activity

Pick a family that is in need. As a family, pray about ways you can help and decide how much money you will spend to put together a gift package. Nonperishable groceries, school supplies, board games, and gift cards are great items to include. Plan an evening to deliver the package. Drive your entire family to the drop-off house and choose someone to make the delivery while you all watch from the car in a hidden parking spot. Place the package on the front porch in secret.

Stress-free Tip

Each time you have to buy school supplies for your children this year, buy at least one extra item and start a collection of items to be included in your secret package for next year. Allow the kids to help pick items out. Try this with canned goods from the store, too. Make sure to check expiration dates before giving as a gift.

Chocolate Dips

(These treats are fun and easy for children to make, plus they make a great gift!)

Melt ½ cup chocolate chips in microwave. Dip any of the following in melted chocolate and let cool on wax paper:

> Graham crackers
> Chocolate sandwich cookies
> Candy canes

Candy canes can be sprinkled with colored sugars and used as cocoa/coffee stirrers. Wrap in cellophane and tie with ribbon.

13 DAYS UNTIL Christmas

How beautiful on the mountains are the feet of those who bring good news, who proclaim peace, who bring good tidings, who proclaim salvation, who say to Zion, "Your God reigns!"
ISAIAH 52:7

Family gatherings seem to be more frequent in December than any other time of year. You'll most likely be around quite a bit of your extended family. Maybe some are Christians who are following the Lord, while others aren't. Decide to be a good example for all of your family members. It's easy to get caught up in family gossip at these large gatherings, but instead, keep your conversations full of good tidings. Be the family member who is always sharing good news and peace with others.

Father, please forgive me for the times that I have gossiped. Help my conversations always to be pleasing to You. In Jesus' name, amen.

Family Activity

Go see *A Christmas Carol* or *The Nutcracker* at a local theater. Many high schools or community theaters will present these or other plays and events for little or no cost. Check your local newspapers for dates and times. Invite grandparents and extended family to join you. If local drama doesn't interest your family, go see a Christmas movie at the movie theater.

Stress-free Tip

Do you need to add anyone to your gift list? Don't forget teachers, neighbors, hair stylists, babysitters, and other people who have done a service for you. These gifts don't have to be pricey—a gift from the oven is an inexpensive gift from the heart!

Vanilla Pecan Crescents

1 cup powdered sugar,
   divided
2 sticks butter
¼ teaspoon salt
2 teaspoons vanilla

1½ cups flour
1¼ cups quick oats
½ cup pecans, finely
   chopped

Preheat oven to 325 degrees. Cream ½ cup sugar into the butter then add the salt and vanilla, blending well. Next add the flour, oats, and nuts, and blend thoroughly. Place dough by the tablespoonful on ungreased cookie sheet. Shape into crescents. Bake for 15 minutes. Remove from pans and sprinkle remaining powdered sugar over the warm crescent cookies.

December 13

12 Days until *Christmas*

"For my thoughts are not your thoughts, neither are your ways my ways," declares the LORD. "As the heavens are higher than the earth, so are my ways higher than your ways and my thoughts than your thoughts."

ISAIAH 55:8–9

Sometimes our carefully laid plans are not God's. Even our very best intentions can end up not being a part of God's plan. Ask Him to help you be flexible in your plans and actions. If things aren't exactly perfect this Christmas or you feel as though something has gone horribly wrong, remember that God has a plan and He will use all things for the good of those who love Him (Romans 8:28).

Dear Lord, thank You for knowing what is best for me. Help me to be flexible when things aren't going my way. Help me to remember that Your plan is perfect. Amen.

Family Activity

Plan a family movie night. Take a trip to the video store and let everyone in your family pick out his or her favorite holiday movie. Serve pizza and popcorn. Break out the sleeping bags, pillows, and pajamas. This would also be a fun night to "camp out" under the Christmas tree and enjoy being together as a family.

Stress-free Tip

If you need to save some money, head to the library instead of the video store and check out Christmas movies there. Borrow Christmas books, too. Spend time each night reading as a family.

JEANNE'S CARAMEL POPCORN

6 cups popped popcorn
2 cups brown sugar
1 cup light corn syrup
1 cup butter

1 teaspoon salt
1 teaspoon vanilla
1 teaspoon soda

Spray large roasting pan with cooking spray. Place popcorn in pan in a 275 degree oven while preparing glaze. In heavy saucepan, combine sugar, corn syrup, butter, and salt. Bring to a boil over medium heat, stirring constantly. Then boil 5 minutes without stirring. Remove from heat. Stir in vanilla and soda. Mixture will be bubbly. Pour over warm popcorn. Stir to coat well. Bake at 375 degree for 45 minutes, stirring occasionally. Cool. Break apart and store in airtight container.

*"Do not store up for yourselves treasures on earth,
where moth and rust destroy, and where thieves break
in and steal. But store up for yourselves treasures
in heaven, where moth and rust do not destroy,
and where thieves do not break in
and steal. For where your treasure is,
there your heart will be also."*
MATTHEW 6:19–21

When you think of your treasure, what comes to mind? Does it consist of temporary, material things, or is it eternal? Jesus tells us to store up our treasure in heaven. This doesn't mean just giving money to your church. Storing up treasure in heaven means giving of yourself, your time, and your talents. Invest yourself in the hearts and lives of your friends and family, your true treasures. This is what has eternal significance!

*Dear Jesus, thank You for reminding us that
our treasure is in heaven. Help me to get my
priorities straight and realize that the treasures that
last for eternity are much more important
than my material things. Amen.*

Family Activity

Plan a game night with family and friends. Find some fun group games online and set out your favorite board games. Have some inexpensive prizes for the winners. To help keep the focus on the spirit of giving, ask guests to bring a nonperishable food item to donate to a local food bank as their entrance fee for game night.

Stress-free Tip

Gift giving can get expensive in large families. Hold a gift exchange with a $10 limit or an exchange in which you must make a gift according to the likes and hobbies of the recipient. For example, if you have a family member who loves watching movies, purchase a large, inexpensive bowl and add a box of microwave popcorn, a few candy bars, several cans of their favorite soda, and a $5 gift card to a video rental store.

Peanut Butter Chocolate Kisses

1 cup butter, softened
1 cup creamy peanut
   butter
1 cup sugar, plus extra
   sugar in a bowl for
   rolling
1 cup brown sugar

2 eggs
2 teaspoons vanilla
3½ cups flour
2 teaspoons baking soda
1 teaspoon salt
1 (16 ounce) package
   chocolate candy kisses

Combine butter, peanut butter, and sugars; blend until creamy. Add eggs and vanilla; blend. Mix flour, soda, and salt; add to cream mixture; mix well. Roll dough into balls and then into a bowl of sugar. Bake at 350 degrees for 7 minutes. Place kiss in the center of the cookie 2 to 3 minutes after removing from the oven.

> O LORD, you have searched me and you know
> me. You know when I sit and when I rise;
> you perceive my thoughts from afar.
> PSALM 139:1–2

Take time to read Psalm 139 as a family. At Christmastime it's easy to leave Jesus in the manger and to think of Him as just a baby. Let Him be real to you. Draw near to Him through these verses. Jesus is the God who knows everything about us and loves us anyway!

Dear Lord, You truly know me inside and out.
These verses remind me that You love me and accept
me and that You want a personal relationship
with me. Thank You for creating me. Amen.

Family Activity

Hold a letter-writing night. First take time to read through Psalm 139. Then write a letter to God telling Him how you feel about what He has to say in these verses. No one else needs to see this letter unless you want to share it. Then write a separate letter to each member of your family. Write something encouraging and tell them what you love about them. If you like, put these letters under the tree until Christmas Day, or share them as soon as you're finished writing.

Stress-free Tip

Make sure to take your gift list with you when you go Christmas shopping. Try to shop on weekdays to avoid the long lines of weekend shoppers. Don't forget to purchase batteries for your camera and for any gifts that might need them.

FAMILY-FAVORITE
CHOCOLATE CHIP COOKIES

⅔ cup shortening
⅔ cup butter
　(no substitutes)
1 cup sugar
1 cup packed brown sugar
2 eggs

2 teaspoons vanilla
3 cups flour
1 teaspoon soda
1 teaspoon salt
2 cups semisweet
　chocolate chips

Heat oven to 375 degrees. Cream shortening, butter, sugars, eggs, and vanilla. Add flour, soda, and salt. Stir in chocolate chips. Drop by tablespoonfuls onto ungreased cookie sheet and bake for 8 minutes or until golden brown.

*I lift up my eyes to the hills—where does my help
come from? My help comes from the LORD,
the Maker of heaven and earth.*
PSALM 121:1–2

It is so amazing to think that the God who made the
heavens and the earth is the same God who loves
us and protects us all the time. He watches over our
comings and goings. He'll be with you during all of
your holiday outings and as you travel the highways
to visit friends and family. We may grow older and
wiser and stronger, but we still need God's protection
each day.

*Dear God, thank You for protecting me. Continue
to watch over us during all of our holiday activities
and road trips. Remind us always that we can never
outgrow our need for You. In Jesus' name, amen.*

Family Activity

If you have a long holiday road trip ahead of you, remember that there are plenty of fun activities to do as a family while you travel. Have one family member pick out several small games to bring along. Have another family member write down a list of questions—some serious, some ridiculous. Take turns asking each other these questions while you travel. Have another family member be in charge of picking out some yummy travel snacks.

Stress-free Tip

It's always wise to buy a few extra gifts just in case you happen to forget someone or someone unexpectedly gives you a gift. Here are some impromptu gift ideas to keep handy: a cookie cutter with your favorite recipe attached, mugs filled with candy, or homemade fudge refrigerated and wrapped.

BANANA CHOCOLATE
CHIP COOKIES

⅔ cup shortening
1 cup sugar
2 eggs
1 teaspoon vanilla
2¼ cups flour
2 teaspoons baking
  powder

½ teaspoon salt
¼ teaspoon baking soda
3 small ripe bananas,
  mashed
1 (12 ounce) package
  milk chocolate chips

Preheat oven to 400 degrees. Blend together shortening
and sugar. Add eggs, beating after each addition. Add
vanilla. Combine dry ingredients and add to cream
mixture. Add mashed bananas and mix well. Stir in
chocolate chips. Drop by teaspoonfuls on ungreased
cookie sheet. Bake for 12 to 15 minutes. Makes 6 dozen.

8 DAYS UNTIL *Christmas*

*Praise the LORD, all you nations; extol him, all
you peoples. For great is his love toward us, and the
faithfulness of the LORD endures forever.
Praise the LORD.*

PSALM 117:1–2

God loves all of us very much. That is why He sent
His only Son to earth as a baby to grow up and save
us from our sins. Christmas is an excellent time to
share God's love with family members, friends, and
neighbors who might not know Him. God's love is
great, and it endures forever! Share that news with
someone this Christmas.

*Dear God, we are amazed at how much You love us.
You are so faithful! We praise You for Your great love
for each one of us. We thank You again and again
for sending Your Son, Jesus, to save us from our
sins. Open many doors for us to share Your
love with others this holiday season. Amen.*

Family Activity

Make family calendars to give away as gifts. Take pictures of each family member around the Christmas tree. Find some current school photos and take some new candids. Make sure each child has equal camera time. If you have a computer program that will make calendars for you, just scan your pictures and print. Or print out blank calendars and glue your pictures on the calendar for each month of the year. Make plenty of copies to give to grandmas, grandpas, and other special relatives or friends.

Stress-free Tip

A great gift for young children to give is a recording of them singing a Christmas song, reading a favorite Christmas book or poem, telling a story, or just saying, "I love you."

EASY CHOCOLATE CRINKLE CAKE MIX COOKIES

1 box chocolate or devil's
    food cake mix
½ cup vegetable oil
2 eggs

1 cup semisweet or
    white chocolate chips
1 cup powdered sugar

Heat oven to 375 degrees. Mix cake mix, vegetable oil, and two eggs until smooth. Stir in chocolate chips. Roll into 1-inch balls and place on ungreased cookie sheet. Bake for 7 minutes or until done. Let cool for 1 minute; then roll in powdered sugar.

*This is the message we have heard from
him and declare to you: God is light;
in him there is no darkness at all.*

1 JOHN 1:5

This year as you admire the twinkling beauty of
Christmas lights, ask the Lord to continually light
up your heart with His love. Confess your sins to
Him and get rid of any darkness that might be
invading your soul. Then listen to the prompting
of the Spirit—pray for someone, call an old friend,
mend a relationship. Even if you assume others know
how much you love them, tell them anyway.

*Dear God, please purify my heart and remove
all of the darkness within me. Let Your light
shine in my soul so that others may see
You living in me. In Jesus' name, amen.*

Family Activity

Take a lights tour! Pop some popcorn and gather some snacks and a thermos of hot cocoa. Drive to several neighborhoods and view Christmas lights after dark. Bundle up so you can see the lights with the car windows down. Bring your camera and take pictures of your favorite displays.

Stress-free Tip

Make and deliver gifts to your neighbors. Some great, no-stress gifts to give your friends next door include cookie trays; homemade breads, fudge, or chocolate-drizzled kettle corn; and homemade crafts.

French Butter Cookies

½ cup butter
½ cup vegetable oil
1½ cups powdered sugar
1 egg
1½ teaspoons vanilla

2 cups flour
1 teaspoon baking soda
1 teaspoon cream of
  tartar

Cream butter, oil, sugar, egg, and vanilla. Beat until thick and creamy. Add dry ingredients. You may want to tint dough with a few drops of red or green food coloring. Chill for at least 2 hours. Shape dough into ¾-inch balls; place on greased cookie sheet about 2 inches apart. Flatten balls with fork and sprinkle with colored sugar. Bake at 350 degrees for 5 to 8 minutes.

"From one man he made every nation of men, that they should inhabit the whole earth; and he determined the times set for them and the exact places where they should live. God did this so that men would seek him and perhaps reach out for him and find him, though he is not far from each one of us."

ACTS 17:26–27

God had already determined where and when we should live long before we were ever born. What a comfort! He knows everything that has happened and will happen to us. His Word says that He is not far from any of us. Like the wise men seeking the baby Jesus so long ago, seek Him, reach out for Him, and you will find Him!

Dear Jesus, help us to remember that You are not far from any of us. Let us seek You each day and reach out for You. Thank You for the promise that we can find You and know You personally! Amen.

Family Activity

Let God's animals enjoy the Christmas season, too. Decorate an animal-friendly tree in your yard just for the birds and squirrels living nearby. Adorn the tree with garland made of popcorn and berries. Roll pinecones in peanut butter and birdseed and hang on the tree.

Stress-free Tip

Don't forget Christmas gifts for your pets. Tie a big bow around a bone, sew some jingle bells on a new collar, or fill a stocking especially for your family pets. These gifts will keep your furry friends occupied and out from underfoot during the activity on Christmas morning.

Laddy's Christmas Puppy Chow (for Humans)

½ cup (1 stick) butter
or margarine
2 cups milk chocolate or
white chocolate chips
1 cup crunchy peanut
butter

1 large box crispy corn
or rice cereal squares
2 cups powdered sugar

In large pot, melt butter, chocolate chips, and peanut butter over medium heat. Remove from heat and add cereal; mix carefully with wooden spoon. Let cool. Measure powdered sugar into large plastic bowl with lid. Add cereal mixture and shake until mixture is evenly coated.

5 DAYS UNTIL *Christmas*

Look to the LORD and his strength;
seek his face always.
1 CHRONICLES 16:11

It's getting down to the wire—just five days until Christmas! Are you relaxed and eager for Christmas Day to arrive? Or are you weary from all of the hustle and bustle? Take some time today to seek the Lord's face. Look to His strength to motivate and inspire all that you do today and in the coming week. Encourage your family members to do the same. Quit worrying over that last batch of cookies that you haven't had time to bake or the floor that hasn't been mopped—seek His face.

Dear Father, help me to seek Your face always.
Help me to rely on Your strength alone during this
busy time and always. In Jesus' name, amen.

Family Activity

Prepare for a relaxing evening at home. Eat dinner together and turn off the TV. Then bring out old photo albums and relive some of the best memories you have as a family. Take turns telling stories about the pictures and events. Then have everyone vote on the top five events in the life of your family so far.

Stress-free Tip

Order takeout tonight to give yourself a break and make this evening as relaxing as possible. Let the kids work on presents for their family members while Mom and Dad have some alone time.

Noel Bars

2 eggs, beaten
1 cup brown sugar
5 tablespoons flour
⅛ teaspoon baking soda
1 cup chopped pecans

1 teaspoon vanilla extract
2 tablespoons melted
  butter
Pinch of cinnamon
Powdered sugar

Preheat oven to 350 degrees. Mix together eggs, brown sugar, flour, baking soda, nuts, and vanilla extract. Pour melted butter into 7x11-inch pan. Top with a pinch of cinnamon. Pour batter over melted butter and cinnamon without stirring. Bake for 20 minutes. Cool, cut into squares, and sprinkle with powdered sugar.

And there were shepherds living out in the fields nearby, keeping watch over their flocks at night. An angel of the Lord appeared to them, and the glory of the Lord shone around them, and they were terrified. But the angel said to them, "Do not be afraid. I bring you good news of great joy that will be for all the people. Today in the town of David a Savior has been born to you; he is Christ the Lord. This will be a sign to you: You will find a baby wrapped in cloths and lying in a manger."

LUKE 2:8–12

Do not be afraid! The holidays can be a time when fear creeps up on us unexpectedly. We can fear for our country, fear the family conflicts that may surface over holiday dinners, fear the state of our finances. . .and the list goes on. The angel said, "Do not be afraid. I bring you good news of great joy that will be for all the people." This season, let your focus be on that joyful news. It's for all of us. Jesus' birth gives us hope. We don't have to fear! John 16:33 says, "In this world you will have trouble. But take heart! I have overcome the world."

Dear Jesus, Thank You that I never have to be afraid. Forgive me for the times I allow myself to worry about things I cannot control. Thank You for bringing us great joy! Amen.

Family Activity

Focus on the good news of great joy. Consider baking a birthday cake for Jesus or putting candles on your favorite dessert or breakfast coffee cake. Don't forget to sing "Happy Birthday" to Him. Remember that we are celebrating the birth of Jesus all month long. Take turns having family members tell why Jesus' birth is important and what it means to them today.

Stress-free Tip

Can't stand the thought of all that wrapping paper being thrown away after packages are opened? Have the kids trace cookie cutters and cut out shapes from the used wrapping paper. You can use the cutouts for scrapbooks and Christmas cards for next year.

Mom's Colossal Christmas Cookies

6 eggs
1 pound brown sugar
2 cups white sugar
½ tablespoon vanilla
½ tablespoon light corn
  syrup
4 teaspoons baking soda
½ pound butter
  (no substitutes)

1½ pounds creamy or
  crunchy peanut butter
9 cups quick oats
½ pound milk chocolate
  chips
½ pound candy-coated
  chocolate pieces

Heat oven to 350 degrees. Mix ingredients in large mixing bowl in the order given. Using an ice cream scoop, drop onto ungreased cookie sheet and flatten with back of scoop or with hand. Drop 6 cookies per sheet. Bake for 10 minutes or until golden brown.

3 DAYS UNTIL *Christmas*

Suddenly a great company of the heavenly host
appeared with the angel, praising God and saying,
"Glory to God in the highest, and on earth peace
to men on whom his favor rests."
LUKE 2:13–14

"Glory to God in the highest!" If we are daily praising God and our hearts are full of love for Him, others cannot help but see the difference He has made in our lives. Worship isn't just about singing songs or Christmas carols at church on Sunday. It's about living life in such a way that is pleasing to God. If we are living a life of worship, we cannot help but tell others about who He is and what He has done for us.

Dear God, help me to live a life of worship
and to give You glory for who You are.
Let my heart be full of love for You. Amen.

Family Activity

Make room in your refrigerator for all of those wonderful Christmas desserts by having a smorgasbord night for dinner! Set out fruit, vegetables, dips, crackers, tortillas, and any leftovers you would like to use up. Let the kids come up with their own creations. Cut food into bite-sized pieces and let everyone snack all evening long. Gather around the table and have fun showing each other your own recipes. Keep the snacks out to munch on while you play a game as a family.

Stress-free Tip

Plan ahead for your Christmas menu and table settings. Purchase mini stockings and place your silverware in them at each place setting. Write names on the stockings with a glitter pen or fabric paint.

Raspberry Oatmeal Bars

½ cup softened butter
½ cup brown sugar
1 cup flour
¼ teaspoon baking
   soda

⅛ teaspoon salt
1 cup quick oats
¾ cup seedless
   raspberry jam

Preheat the oven to 350 degrees. Mix all the ingredients together, except the jam. Press 2 cups of the mixture into the bottom of a greased 8-inch pan. Spread the jam to within ¼ inch of the edge. Sprinkle the remaining crumb mixture over the top and lightly press it into the jam. Bake 35 to 40 minutes and allow to cool before cutting into bars.

DECEMBER 23

2 Days until Christmas

*So they hurried off and found Mary and Joseph, and
the baby, who was lying in the manger. When they had
seen him, they spread the word concerning what had
been told them about this child, and all who heard it
were amazed at what the shepherds said to them.
But Mary treasured up all these things and
pondered them in her heart.*
LUKE 2:16–19

Make time to treasure your family this Christmas.
Watch as family members interact with each other.
Take joy in their facial expressions and feelings.
Whenever you feel tired or stressed with nothing left
to give, pray for strength and remember that the days
may seem long, but the years go by quickly. Try not
to miss a minute of it, and ponder all these things in
your own heart.

*Dear Jesus, thank You for each of my family
members. Please give me strength and patience
when I feel overwhelmed by the stresses of life.
Help me to take time to treasure my family. Amen.*

Family Activity

Have each family member make special coupons for each other. Parents can make coupons for individual "date nights" with the kids. Spouses can make coupons for breakfast in bed or a foot massage. Children can make coupons for washing the dishes, cleaning the house, mowing the lawn, making the bed for a parent or sibling, and so forth. Each family member should receive at least one coupon from every member of your family in a decorated envelope.

Stress-free Tip

Relax and enjoy the sights and sounds of the holiday season. Christmas specials are on TV, the refrigerator is filled with goodies, and all your holiday planning is complete! Thank God for your family and friends and this special time together.

CHOCOLATE
CHRISTMAS PIZZA

1 tube refrigerated
  chocolate chip cookie
  dough
½ cup creamy or crunchy
  peanut butter
1 cup milk chocolate
  chips

3 favorite candy bars,
  chopped
1 (single serving) bag
  candy-coated chocolate
  pieces
Red and green sprinkles

Press refrigerated cookie dough into round pizza pan. Bake as directed on package or until almost done in the middle but not too brown. Let cool for 2 minutes. Spread peanut butter over cookie crust and sprinkle with chocolate chips. Wait for 2 or 3 minutes until peanut butter and chocolate chips start to melt; then spread evenly over cookie crust. Decorate with chopped candy bars, candy-coated chocolate pieces, and sprinkles.

*The shepherds returned, glorifying and praising
God for all the things they had heard and seen,
which were just as they had been told.*
LUKE 2:20

The shepherds found Jesus and realized that the
angel's words to them were true. "A Savior has been
born to you; he is Christ the Lord" (Luke 2:11).
They were glorifying and praising God because their
Savior had been born! They had seen the face of God
and were forever changed. The God of the universe
came as a baby to save them. . .and to save us.

*Dear Jesus, open our hearts to see You as You are.
You are the God of all creation who came
as a baby to save us. We give You
glory and honor. Amen.*

Family Activity

Attend a candlelight Christmas Eve service with your family. If your church doesn't have a service by candlelight, look in the papers and call other churches in your area. If you can't find one, hold a candlelight service at home. Light as many candles as you can find and sing some Christmas carols as a family. Don't forget to read the Christmas story from the Bible (found in Matthew 1 and Luke 2).

Stress-free Tip

Make it your goal for Christmas Day to be as relaxing and fun as possible. One way to achieve this goal is to have everything ready to go the night before. Cut up vegetables needed for casseroles, brown the sausage, set the table, fill the stockings, and assemble all the toys.

Almond Roca Bars

1 cup butter
½ cup sugar
½ cup brown sugar
1 egg, beaten
1 teaspoon vanilla
½ teaspoon almond
   extract

2 cups minus 2
   tablespoons flour
1 (12 ounce) bag of
   chocolate chips
1 small package slivered
   or roasted almonds

Preheat oven to 350 degrees. Cream together butter and sugars. Add egg, vanilla, almond extract, and flour. Mix thoroughly and spread on large cookie sheet. Bake for 10 to 12 minutes. Melt chocolate chips in microwave for 30 seconds. Stir. Repeat until creamy. Spread over warm cookie and then sprinkle slivered almonds on top. Cut into bars when cooled.

Christmas Day

> *All this took place to fulfill what the Lord had said*
> *through the prophet: "The virgin will be with child*
> *and will give birth to a son, and they will call him*
> *Immanuel"—which means, "God with us."*
> MATTHEW 1:22–23

Jesus had many names: Jehovah, King of kings, Prince of peace, Jesus Christ, Messiah, the Word, and many more. Another name of Jesus is Immanuel, which means "God with us." God came to us as a baby, and He continues to live in our hearts today. He will never leave us or abandon us! (Hebrews 13:5). Remember the meaning as you sing "Immanuel" in many Christmas carols this season.

Dear Jesus, happy birthday!
We are celebrating You today. Help us to
remember in all of our festivities today
that we are the reason that You came. Amen.

Family Activity

Have a grandparent or other family member take a picture of your immediate family. Turn this picture into an ornament and personalize it with your last name and the date. Make this a tradition each year. These personalized ornaments will be treasured family heirlooms for years to come.

As you are opening and enjoying presents, eating fabulous food, and spending time with your family, don't forget to thank God for all that He has given you. If you wrote letters to each other on December 15, make time to read them today. Have a wonderful day as a family! Merry Christmas!

Stress-free Tip

Let young children open their presents first; then take turns with older children and adults opening presents one by one. This way you can enjoy watching family members' faces as they open their gifts—and the festivities last a lot longer!

CHRISTMAS MORNING CASSEROLE

2 tubes refrigerated
  crescent rolls
2 tablespoons butter
1 small onion, chopped
1 green pepper, chopped

½ cup mushrooms
8 eggs
1 package sausage links
2 cups shredded cheddar
  cheese

Preheat oven according to crescent roll package directions. Press crescent rolls into 9x12-inch pan, pressing halfway up sides. Melt butter in saucepan. Sauté onion, green pepper, and mushrooms in butter. Remove from saucepan and set aside. In same saucepan, scramble eggs. Meanwhile, in separate pan, brown sausage links. Cool and cut into small pieces. Layer eggs, mushrooms, onion, green pepper, sausage, and cheese on top of crescent roll crust. Bake as directed on crescent roll package or until done.

1 DAY AFTER Christmas

After Jesus was born in Bethlehem in Judea,
during the time of King Herod, Magi from the east
came to Jerusalem and asked, "Where is the one who
has been born king of the Jews? We saw his star
in the east and have come to worship him."

MATTHEW 2:1–2

The wise men traveled many miles to worship Jesus. They went out of their way to find Him and bring gifts to Him. Do you ever go out of your way to worship the Lord? Do you worship even when it isn't convenient for you? God is worthy of our worship whether we feel like worshipping or not. If you've had a rough week, aren't feeling well, or feel really stressed about something, remember that God is still worthy of your worship. When we worship God even when we don't feel like it, He allows us to see Him, and our problems look much smaller in His presence!

Dear God, help me to worship You even when
I don't feel like it. You are worthy of all my
worship, all the time! In Jesus' name, amen.

Family Activity

Spend some one-on-one time with each family member today. Have breakfast with your daughter by the Christmas tree; have lunch with your son on a quilt in the living room; have dessert with your spouse in the kitchen; and so forth. Ask family members to tell you what they loved about Christmas this year. What were their favorite gifts? With whom did they have the best conversation over the holidays? What was it about? What was their favorite dessert? What was something new they'd never done before? What have they learned from daily devotions?

Stress-free Tip

Don't like the excitement of Christmas ending after one day? Celebrate the twelve days of Christmas! Open most of the gifts on Christmas Day, but save twelve small gifts for the next two weeks to make Christmas last longer. These gifts can be as simple as a favorite candy bar sitting on a dinner plate or a pack of stickers left on a nightstand.

Magic Nutty Bars

½ cup butter
1½ cups graham cracker
   crumbs
1 (14 ounce) can
   sweetened condensed
   milk

1 (6 ounce) package
   semisweet chocolate
   chips
1⅓ cups flaked coconut
1 cup chopped pecans
   or peanuts

Preheat oven to 350 degrees. Melt butter in a 9x13-inch baking pan. Sprinkle crumbs evenly over melted butter; pour sweetened condensed milk evenly over crumbs. Top evenly with remaining ingredients; press down firmly with a fork. Bake for 25 minutes or until lightly browned. Cool and cut into bars.

2 DAYS AFTER *Christmas*

But in your hearts set apart Christ as Lord.
Always be prepared to give an answer to
everyone who asks you to give the reason
for the hope that you have.
1 PETER 3:15

Every baby born is a miracle from God. But when the baby Jesus was born, everyone who came to see Him knew that this baby was different. The shepherds and the wise men came to worship Jesus. They knew in their hearts the baby was Christ the Lord. Just as the shepherds spread the word about Jesus (Luke 2:17), we should be prepared to tell others why we set apart Christ as Lord. If we live by faith and hope, people will notice and want to know why we are different. Be ready to give them an answer that pleases the Lord!

Dear Jesus, help me to be prepared to answer
questions about my faith and to be willing
to share my love for You with others. Amen.

Family Activity

Make it a point to have family night at least twice a month this coming year. Have family members take turns planning the activity and the menu. Even your youngest ones will have something to contribute. One time a month, have a surprise guest night. The event planner can invite one or two secret guests whom the whole family will enjoy having over—Grandma and Grandpa, a cousin, a Sunday school teacher, and so on. The rest of the family can take turns asking questions to try to guess who is coming.

Stress-free Tip

Don't forget those after-Christmas sales! Check ads in the newspaper to find out which stores are having 50- to 75-percent-off sales. This is a great time to stock up and save for next year! Make sure to label your boxes well before you put these gifts into storage so you don't forget that you already have gifts for next Christmas.

Gramma Karen's Peanut Butter Pie

⅓ cup peanut butter
¾ cup powdered sugar
1 prebaked pie shell

1 large box cook-and-serve vanilla pudding
2 cups frozen whipped topping, thawed

In small bowl, use pastry blender to combine peanut butter and powdered sugar. Set aside. Line prebaked pie shell (refrigerated or homemade) with one-third of peanut butter mixture. Make vanilla pudding according to package directions and spread over peanut butter mixture. Cool. Top with whipped topping and sprinkle with remaining peanut butter mixture. Chill well before serving.

3 DAYS AFTER *Christmas*

"The God who made the world and everything in it is the Lord of heaven and earth and does not live in temples built by hands. And he is not served by human hands, as if he needed anything, because he himself gives all men life and breath and everything else."

ACTS 17:24–25

Our God is the Lord of heaven and earth. God's Word says that He doesn't live in temples built by human hands. He is the living God who resides in our hearts. He doesn't need us to serve Him, but He wants us to. We shouldn't serve Him because we feel guilty. Instead, we should serve Him as an act of worship to the God who gave us life and breath and everything else. Whether it is serving as a prayer partner at church, rocking babies in the nursery, welcoming people as they walk into the worship center, playing the keyboard for the worship team, or serving a meal at the local soup kitchen, there is a place for everyone in your family to serve!

Dear Jesus, please show us how we can serve You. Give us the desire in our hearts to please You and to serve You with willing and grateful hearts. Amen.

Family Activity

God has given each of us spiritual gifts to share. Sit down as a family and try to figure out what each of your gifts are. Ask what your spouse and your kids feel passionate about. What are their strengths and weaknesses? Be honest with one another about this topic, and encourage each other in your gifts and talents. Discuss ways to get involved in your local church and missions.

Stress-free Tip

Instead of throwing away all of the beautiful Christmas cards you received this year, save them! Keep them by your Bible and pray for a different family each day. You can also cut them into gift tags for next year, make them into Christmas ornaments, use them in scrapbooks, or create new cards out of them.

Chocolate Candy
Caramel Bars

1 box chocolate cake
  with pudding mix
½ cup shortening
1 cup evaporated milk,
  divided

1 package soft caramels
1 (14 ounce) bag candy-
  coated chocolate pieces

Preheat oven to 350 degrees. Grease 9x12-inch pan. Combine cake mix, shortening, and ⅔ cup evaporated milk. Mix well. Spread half of the batter in pan. Bake 15 minutes. Combine caramels and ⅓ cup evaporated milk and heat in microwave until smooth. Sprinkle 1 cup candy-coated chocolate pieces over batter. Drizzle with caramel mixture. Spoon remaining batter over caramel. Add remaining candy-coated chocolate pieces. Bake 25 minutes. Cool. Cut into bars.

4 DAYS AFTER *Christmas*

But I trust in you, O Lord; I say,
"You are my God." My times are in your hands.
PSALM 31:14–15

Lord, I hide myself in You.
You are my rock; You are my refuge.
Lead me; guide me. Walk beside me.
All my times are in Your hands.
You know exactly what I am.
Lead me; guide me. Walk beside me.

You are my refuge. Sometimes I run to You and
hide. You make all things new. I put my hope in
You.Come to my rescue. Sometimes I need a place
to cry, A safe place of rest to come to. The place
where I find You.

Dear Lord, thank You that all of my times are in
Your hands. You are my refuge and I trust in You.
Lead me and guide me as I enter another year.
In Jesus' name, amen.

Family Activity

Plan a family council night. Prepare your family's favorite meal and dessert. Let family members know ahead of time that they will be included in the discussion—everyone gets a say at family council! Ask questions such as the following: Are we spending enough time together as a family? Are we eating dinner together often enough throughout the week? What is important to each child? Talk about what each family member was thankful for this past year. Allow all members to share their goals for the coming year. Plan activities for your entire family to do in the next three months.

Stress-free Tip

During family council night, write down all the answers you receive from your children and your spouse in a notebook and date them. Use this same notebook each year. Go through the notebook throughout the year and check to make sure everyone's needs are being met and goals are being accomplished.

BERRY PATCH CARAMEL

2⅔ cups brown sugar
1 cup light corn syrup
1 (14 ounce) can sweetened
  condensed milk
1 cup butter
1 teaspoon vanilla

In saucepan, bring brown sugar, corn syrup, sweetened condensed milk, and butter to a boil, stirring constantly until temperature reaches 245 degrees, or firm ball stage. Remove from heat and add vanilla. Pour into greased 9x9-inch pan. Cool. Cut into squares and wrap in cellophane.

5 DAYS AFTER *Christmas*

Cast all your anxiety on him
because he cares for you.
1 PETER 5:7

It is such a relief to know that God cares for us and wants to take away all of our worries. In Luke 12:22, Jesus tells us not to worry. This isn't just advice or a suggestion; it is a command. As we approach a brand-new year, many challenges lie ahead. Ask the Lord to help you keep your focus on Him and deal with one thing at a time. He cares for you and wants to help you.

Dear heavenly Father, so many things are on my mind
right now. Please help me to focus on You and trust
that You will help me deal with things as they come.
Thank You for caring for me so much. Amen

Family Activity

Plan a "take down the tree" party with your family. Play festive music, have some refreshments handy, and start undecorating. Hang a special ornament in a hidden spot on your tree or in your house somewhere. As your family is cleaning up, the first one to find the special ornament gets a prize! You might even want to keep a few small gifts hidden under the tree for your children to find as they help take down the tree. This surprise makes a depressing job a lot more fun!

Stress-free Tip

Check to see if your city recycles Christmas trees. If not, call a business that grinds stumps and ask them to turn your tree into mulch. You also could cut off the branches and lay them over your potted flowers or flower beds to protect them from a harsh winter. Some people also sink evergreen trees in large ponds or lakes as a refuge for fish.

CHINESE NEW YEAR COOKIES

½ cup semisweet chocolate chips
½ cup butterscotch chips
1 (3 ounce) can Chinese noodles
1 (7 ounce) can salted peanuts

Heat chocolate and butterscotch chips in microwave for 1 minute on high. Stir. Continue heating for 30 seconds at a time until chips are smooth. Mix in noodles and nuts. Drop by teaspoonfuls onto wax paper. Chill. Makes about 4 dozen cookies.

December 31

*"For I know the plans I have for you," declares the
LORD, "plans to prosper you and not to harm you,
plans to give you hope and a future. Then you will call
upon me and come and pray to me, and I will listen
to you. You will seek me and find me when
you seek me with all your heart."*

JEREMIAH 29:11–13

These are wonderful verses to help us remember our
purpose in life. As we enter the new year this evening,
remember that God has good plans for our lives. He
wants to give us a hope and a future. We also have
the promise of finding God when we seek Him with
all our hearts. Make that your goal and desire from
this day forward. Commit personally and as a family
to seeking the Lord each day.

*Dear Lord, You already know the plans You have
for me. Help me to seek You each day so that I can
discover Your plan for my life. Thank You for
Your promises. Thank You for always being
faithful to us. In Jesus' name, amen.*

Family Activity

Plan a progressive dinner for New Year's Eve. Call up family and friends and decide which family will host the appetizer, the soup or salad, the main course, and the dessert. Drive to one home for the appetizer, another home for the soup or salad, and so on. This helps share the cost and responsibility of an otherwise expensive and large party. Watch the ball drop and ring in the New Year at the last home!

Stress-free Tip

Take time for a brisk walk this afternoon. Bundle up and get as many family members as you can to join you. Walking is a great energizer, does much to lift the spirits, and helps work off the extra calories from all those delicious Christmas cookies. Have a happy New Year!

Easy New Year's Meatballs

20–25 precooked
  frozen meatballs
1 cup ketchup
¾ cup packed brown
  sugar

½ cup chopped onion
¼ teaspoon garlic powder
⅛ teaspoon
  Worcestershire sauce

Stovetop directions: Combine all ingredients in large pot. Cook over medium-high heat for 15 to 20 minutes.

Slow cooker directions: Combine all ingredients in slow cooker. Cook on low for 3 to 4 hours.